gaudí
of Barcelona

gaudí
of Barcelona

Adapted from the Spanish text by **Lluís Permanyer**
Photographs **Melba Levick**

Ediciones Polígrafa, S.A.

Photographic Credits

Arxiu Dr. Comas Llaberia, pp. 11 and 14.
Arxiu Nacional de Catalunya. Fons Brangulí, p. 6.
Francesc Català-Roca, p. 17.
Museu Comarcal Salvador Vilaseca, Reus, p. 185.
Pere Vivas, pp. 15, 125 and 150 above.

*The publishers and authors would also like to express their gratitude
to the following individuals and institutions who have permitted
photographs to be taken of the buildings reproduced in this book:*
Casa Batlló
Càtedra Gaudí
Col·legi de Santa Teresa de Jesús
Diputació de Barcelona
Fundació Caixa de Catalunya
Lluís Guilera Soler
Fabiola Jover de Herrero
Junta Constructora del Temple de la Sagrada Família
Santiago Llensa Boyer
Parròquia del Sagrat Cor, Santa Coloma de Cervelló

I.S.B.N.: 84-343-0839-8
D. L.: B. 22.838 - 1997 (Printed in Spain)

Colour separations by Alfacrom, Barcelona
Printed by Filabo, S. A., Sant Joan Despí (Barcelona)

The Man and the City

Gaudí was fortunate to have lived at a time in which he received the patronage of clients who gave him a great deal of latitude, financially and aesthetically, to produce audacious and often unorthodox work. He caught the attention of prominent members of a bourgeoisie that enjoyed ever-increasing prosperity, self-confident men who wanted to distinguish themselves in every way possible. These successful merchants and industrialists found in architecture not only a form of investment, but also a significant and visible medium through which to convey their identity.

Gaudí also had the freedom to explore a variety of building types, from residential to ecclesiastical, without the scope of his vision being restricted by site limitations. I cannot help imagining how different his work might have been in the densely populated Barcelona of a few decades earlier, crammed as it was inside the city walls. Projects such as Park Güell, the Sagrada Família church, and Casa Milà would never have been created. We might also wonder whether in the narrow streets of the walled city he would have conceived facades such as that of Casa Batlló, which was intended to be seen from a distance. At the time Gaudí was receiving commissions, Ildefons Cerdà was planning the city extension laid out on the grid system, which made more land available for development in Barcelona than in any other major European city at the time. Wealthy individuals and their architects had at their disposal areas previously outside the city's perimeter, and thus the astonishing spectacle of the area of Barcelona known as the Eixample took shape.

This was also the period when Catalonia had firmly embarked on the recovery of its political independence, of which it had been deprived in 1714 by Philip V when the Catalans sided with his chief rival, the Archduke Charles, in the War of Spanish Succession. Central to this movement, known as the *Renaixença*, was a search for a strong regional identity, and it brought about a cultural and economic resurgence.

There are those who believe that Gaudí was lucky to have been practising during the height of *Modernisme*, the artistic and architectural style that was the Catalan version of the Art Nouveau and Jugendstil movements; personally, I am not so sure. I do not believe that Gaudí could be labelled a *modernista* architect. He certainly benefitted from having lived in a period of such splendour and creative fervour, above all in the applied arts, as he was able to collaborate with extremely talented artists and craftsmen. Some of his work does express *modernista* characteristics, but his unorthodox and inventive design solutions defy such categorisation.

Antoni Gaudí i Cornet was born on June 25, 1852. While it is still not certain whether he came into this world in Reus or in Riudoms, a small village only four kilometres from the city, documentary evidence points to Reus. Natives of this region were said to be "*Gent del Camp, gent del llamp* (People from El Camp, people of lightning)." Strength, determination, obstinacy, and tenacity were among their traits, and these were certainly characteristics of Gaudí's personality. Throughout his architectural career he acted as a true *reusenc*, making no concessions regarding his aesthetic beliefs, despite conflicts that arose with clients, critics, and the press; in fact, much of society at the time did not understand or appreciate his artistic vision. He staunchly stood his ground in the face of incomprehension and opposition, and his architecture was eventually accepted. On one occasion he claimed that he had managed to overcome all of his defects save one: his irascibility.

I believe that, as his career evolved, he positively cultivated it.

Gaudí's father was a coppersmith, and the architect claimed he was thus endowed with a sense of space that gave him the ability to think directly in three dimensions, which was less restrictive than the two dimensions used when drawing up plans.

An event of capital importance took place in 1869: he was sent to a school in Barcelona to complete his secondary education. From that moment onwards, Gaudí made his home in the city that provided him with the opportunity to make contacts, gain access to valuable sources of information, and meet artisans with whom he would collaborate and businessmen who would become his clients and patrons. Here, too, he had at his disposal sites on which he could transform his dreams into buildings that would occupy their rightful place in the history of world architecture.

Both at secondary school and at the Escola d'Arquitectura, Gaudí excelled in some disciplines while declaring himself uninterested in or incapable of understanding others, to the extent that one of his professors declared that he did not know whether he was in the presence of a genius or a lunatic. Gaudí had serious problems with spelling and proved to be only a mediocre draughtsman. Moreover, he was a pupil who did not recognise his teachers as masters and dared to contradict them. This gives us an early glimpse of the architect who would become known for his cutting rejoinders to powerful and influential people.

After completing his studies, Gaudí worked as a draughtsman for Francesc de Paula del Villar,

from whom he acquired no great knowledge, and who, ironically, he replaced as the architect of Sagrada Família. He also collaborated with Josep Fontserè, a professional he esteemed and respected, in whose studio he contributed to the realisation of certain details of the Ciutadella Park. Perhaps the architect who had the most influence on him was Joan Martorell, with whom Gaudí worked on a number of important Barcelona projects, such as the Jesuit church in Carrer de Casp and the Salesian convent in Passeig de Sant Joan. Martorell later recommended that Gaudí take over as architect of Sagrada Família.

Gaudí also came in contact with consummate craftsmen such as Eudald Puntí, a master of the hammer and fire who transformed iron into art. It was in Puntí's workshop that Gaudí designed one of his first projects, a display cabinet for a collection of gloves by designer Esteve Comellas. It was exhibited at the 1878 Exposition Universelle in Paris, where it deeply impressed none other than Eusebi Güell, who ultimately became one of Gaudí's most important patrons. Güell was so moved by the piece that he would not rest until he had met the artist. An appreciation for the work led to a fascination with its creator, and a lifelong friendship evolved from the meeting, which took place in Puntí's atelier.

This encounter between Gaudí and Güell was providential, not only for the commissions that resulted, significant in their scope and diversity, but also for the complete trust Güell placed in his architect, and for the freedom in which he allowed him to work. As a result of Güell's patronage, the haute bourgeoisie came to know his young protégé and his work. Gaudí became a public figure, often featured in press, despite his prickly, solitary nature. He was completely devoted to his work, which was the only thing that interested him.

When the Palau Güell was under construction it was the object of much speculation and curiosity. At that time, Carrer Nou de la Rambla was one of the city's busiest locations, with the famous Edèn Concert just opposite the palace. One day Gaudí and Güell were observing the effect produced by the great wrought iron representation of the Catalan coat of arms which stood between the two entrance doors, when someone uttered a loudly pejorative remark. The owner's immediate rejoinder was, "Well, now I like it more!" The Palau Güell provoked many barbed witticisms. As the vaulted basement took shape, writer and painter Santiago Rusiñol wrote that Babylonian remains had been found there. Even the serious respected daily *La Vanguardia* printed an *innocentada*, or practical joke, on the Catalan equivalent of April Fool's Day, stating that a dungeon and lion's cage from the days of Balthasar or Nebuchadnezzar had been discovered on the site. Once the impressive building had been completed, the satirical magazine *¡Cu-cut!* published a cartoon of the facade, with the caption an exchange between two astonished citizens: "This looks like a jail," comments one. "No, it's the house of a gentleman," his friend replies.

Although Park Güell was a huge project, it was incomplete and relatively remote, thus provoking more moderate reactions from commentators and cartoonists. The satirical publication *L'Esquella*, however, observed that, while in one corner of the park a group of workmen were smashing tiles, a short distance away another team was engaged in the laborious task of reconstructing the jigsaw puzzle.

Gaudí had the courage of his convictions and refused to be put off by others' reactions. He became known for his acerbic rejoinders to comments he considered insolent, and his facial expressions reflected his disdain. The painter Porcar recalls that "his eyes resembled those of the tiger in the zoo." When a pedantic young man expressed his irritation at one of the architect's works, Gaudí replied, "I'm not doing it to please you." And when an insensitive woman asked him what the obstacles were on top of the balls that crowned Casa Calvet,

his ironic reply was, "The cross, madam, which for some is indeed an obstacle."

Needless to say, Casa Batlló also caused quite a stir. By the turn of the century, Passeig de Gràcia had become the city's grandest avenue. It was like an open-air salon where the best of Barcelona society gathered to stroll and be seen. An indication of the competitive climate of the period was the fact that Milà, on seeing the unique residence Gaudí had designed for his friend and business partner Batlló, promptly commissioned him to build an apartment building on an even more visible site. The brilliant architect was quick to take advantage of the offer, and set to work at once. The press reflected public opinion early on, as some of the cartoons show Casa Milà, or La Pedrera, surrounded by works barriers. The building was characterised as a hangar for Zeppelins, an Easter cake, and the result of an earthquake. The metal guardrails designed by Gaudí's talented collaborator Josep Maria Jujol were also the object of derision. In one cartoon an alarmed citizen asked if the twisted metal wreckage of a railway accident had been used for the project. A prospective tenant refused to rent one of the flats because he would be unable to hang out the banners for the Corpus Christi celebrations. Attacks were directed not only at the architect, but also the owner. The most pompous members of the bourgeoisie who resided in the Passeig de Gràcia snubbed the Milà family, indicating that they felt the construction of La Pedrera had caused

irreparable damage to the prestige of such a noble district. Milà also became the butt of malicious jokes concerning his second marriage to the wealthy Guardiola widow, as a *guardiola* is a moneybox in Catalan.

Prosperous members of the bourgeoisie were eager to broadcast their financial success and social position by constructing impressive buildings in the Eixample district. In *Modernisme*, architects found the freedom to break away from traditional styles and create projects that would not have been tolerated in the past. Clients sought out architects who could provide them with unique designs that would distinguish them from their neighbours and competitors. In this Güell surpassed all rivals, thanks to his ongoing collaboration with Gaudí.

Gaudí was so self-assured and committed to executing his designs without intervention from clients or bureaucrats that he ignored not only criticism but also building codes. The municipal architect Rovira i Trias refused to approve the plans for the Palau Güell; Casa Calvet was higher than regulations allowed; work on Casa Batlló was halted, as it had begun without authorisation; the dimensions of Casa Milà exceeded permitted limits, and a column at street level blocked pedestrian traffic. Unfazed by these issues, the architect responded in each case by confronting the authorities. It must be said that government officials ultimately tolerated his excesses and made exceptions to accommodate Gaudí's designs.

The people of Barcelona felt they were living in a state of grace after centuries of repression and decline. They secretly admired the controversy inspired by such a genius as Gaudí, and thrived in a city that was exploding with new life and a new freedom of expression. People

LA CASA-PEDRERA

— Està bé, tot m'agrada, però no us puc llogar el pis!
— Per què?
— Perquè amb aquestes baranes tan artistiques no em seria possible mai posar domassos als balcons.

from outside, however, were not prepared for such excesses. An individual from Granada who purchased a *modernista* house in Barcelona put up a sign saying: "The present owner is not responsible for this facade." Unamuno fired off insults, writing that the urban landscape of Barcelona was *fachadosa*, or facade-infested. From as far away as New York, Juan Ramón Jiménez described *modernista* Barcelona as "the victim of a Catalan architect's nightmare." Valle Inclán, indignant at the sight of the Palau Güell, described it in one of his novels as "funereal, barbarous, and Catalan."

In 1910, Clemenceau, the French Prime Minister, made a brief stopover in Barcelona on his way back to Paris from South America. He ordered a hackney carriage and asked to be driven up the Passeig de Gràcia, where he was particularly shocked by the facade of Casa Milà, La Pedrera, commenting later, "Horrible! In Barcelona they are building houses for dinosaurs and dragons!" Rusiñol had said that the only pets suitable for La Pedrera were snakes. When, in the seventies, the Parisian art dealer Maeght decided to open a gallery in Barcelona, he was tempted at first

to install it on the first floor of La Pedrera, but changed his mind when he realised that with so many curved walls and partitions it would be impossible to hang pictures for an exhibition.

Writer and cartoonist Apel·les Mestres commented that whenever a prospective client approached Gaudí, he would reply that before accepting the commission he would have to consult the Virgin Mary. Mestres added, "Unfortunately for the good name of Catalan architecture, the Virgin always told him to go ahead!" He also recounted that architect Domènech i Montaner had told him this anecdote: One day Gaudí was entrusted with the design of a pitcher. The architect racked his brains as to what the most suitable material would be until, at last, he chose wire netting!

Gaudí and the advocates and practitioners of *Modernisme* had to endure the scorn of the militants of *Noucentisme*, the early twentieth-century cultural and political movement that advocated a return to classicism and traditional Catalan values. *Noucentistes* declared their hatred of *Modernisme* claiming they felt physical discom-

In Junceda's biting cartoon published in ¡Cu-cut!, in 1910, the child exclaims, "Daddy, Daddy, I want a big Easter cake like that one!"

According to this cartoon published in L'Esquella de la Torratxa in 1912, the building would eventually become a multi-storey zeppelin garage.

fort in the presence of its works and calling for their demolition. Today it is hard to believe that action would be taken on the recommendations of such a radical group, but many important examples of an architectural style that had provided Catalan culture with its greatest splendour since Gothic times were destroyed. Even the Palau de la Música Catalana was threatened. Numerous buildings that remained standing were ignobly mutilated. In one of the most tragic cases, Arnau's sculpture, which embellished the ground-floor facade of Casa Lleó i Morera at no. 35, Passeig de Gràcia, was removed. This outrage was committed by architect Raimon Duran i Reynals, a *noucentista*, needless to say. It is difficult to believe that such destruction could be carried out by educated, cultured people; however, as Gustave Flaubert noted, ''Bad taste is the taste of the generation before,'' and *noucentistes* sought to eradicate the *Modernisme* which had preceded them.

Although he was not, strictly speaking, a *modernista*, Gaudí belonged to that generation, and suffered many of the consequences of the campaign. In fact, his radically avant-garde concepts were the object of even greater ridicule. As I have stated before, he was so committed to his artistic principles and sure of his direction that this criticism rolled off his back. He increasingly removed himself from the hubbub of worldly life, beginning in about 1911 and devoted himself body and soul to the Temple of the Sagrada Família, even living on the site during his last years. I believe that ill health precipitated this withdrawal, as in 1910 he suffered a deep depression, followed by anaemia, which rendered him defenceless against Maltese fever. His condition was so serious that he dictated his last will and testament. I suspect that he decided he had produced a sufficient body of work and could

— Ja és estrany que no la cremessin.
— Oh, és que no estava acabada.

The painter and cartoonist Martí Bas, in L'Esquella *in 1937, suggested that the anarchists had not burnt down the Sagrada Família because it was still unfinished.*

—¿Què vols que't digui? a n'aquet temple no li veig la punta.
—¡Y tantes que'n té!

The cartoonist Opisso, who eventually became one of Gaudí's admirers, scoffed at the Sagrada Família in the calendar published by ¡Cu-cut! *in 1907.*

refuse further commissions in order to concentrate on the "folly" of the Sagrada Família. In some ways, this was unfortunate, as he was mature and experienced enough to develop the technical solutions demanded by his increasingly innovative project concepts. His achievements in this regard were gaining respect. In 1915 members of the Escola d'Arquitectura de Barcelona commented on the brilliance of certain structural solutions he was applying at the time. In those academic circles his work was considered revolutionary.

Death came upon Gaudí suddenly. One afternoon he was walking, as was his custom, to the Church of Sant Felip Neri to pray when he was run over by a tram while crossing the Granvia near Carrer Bailèn. Because of his ragged

appearance, he was not recognised or given the emergency treatment he required. He died three days later in the Hospital de la Santa Creu. He was buried in the Sagrada Família, the church to which he had devoted no fewer than forty-three years of his life.

Shortly after the outbreak of the Civil War in 1936, *L'Esquella* published a pencil drawing by Martí Bas, featuring the following exchange between two citizens of Barcelona: One declares himself to be astonished to see that the Sagrada Família had not fallen victim to revolutionary arsonists; the other replies, "Oh, that's because it hasn't been finished." Humour aside, I very much fear that some would have been overjoyed to witness the destruction of such an unorthodox work of architecture. Apart from Güell, his artistic collaborators, and a few critics such as Ràfols or Pujols, I feel that none of his contemporaries believed in Gaudí's genius. At best he was respected as an imaginative eccentric. When his work was exhibited in the Grand Palais in Paris in 1910 Gaudí was praised but misunderstood for both aesthetic and religious reasons. Some of the works shown were exhibited the following year at the first Salón de la Arquitectura in the Retiro, Madrid, organised by the Associació d'Arquitectes de Catalunya. Salvador Dalí deserves recognition as Gaudí's first staunch defender; he perceived the scope and rarity of the architect's genius as no one had before. Thanks to Dalí, Surrealists such as Breton, Crevel, and Cocteau became aware of his work and spread the word throughout the most revolutionary international cultural circles. The 1929 Barcelona World Exposition also provided travellers and writers, including Evelyn Waugh, with the opportunity to marvel at Gaudí's work. His first champion among architects was, perhaps, Le Corbusier, whose reputation in avant-garde circles undoubtedly contributed to a just appraisal of the Catalan's work.

Nonetheless, international awareness of Gaudí's genius did not come until 1952, when American historian George R. Collins presented a major exhibition of his work in New York. The Japanese have since expressed a boundless passion and fascination for Gaudí. Ironically, recognition of Gaudí's contributions to the field of architecture have led to a re-evaluation in recent years of the merits of *Modernisme*, a movement with which he was only loosely associated. Recognition on a more popular level of both Gaudí and the *Modernistes* came with the 1992 Olympic Games in Barcelona. Today, Gaudí's work is known and admired all over the world, and the image of Barcelona is inextricably linked to his work.

Early Works

The earliest of Gaudí's extant works are the street lamps he designed in 1878 for the Plaça Reial. Two examples of the six-branched version were erected on the occasion of the Mercè festivities that year. The cast iron and bronze lamp posts stand on stone pedestals, and are crowned with helmets evoking the god Mercury. In the Plaça Palau a pair of three-branched lamps, with inverted crowns replacing the helmets, have flanked the side entrance to the Civil Governor's Palace since 1889. At one time a civil governor ordered the removal of the crowns, as he perceived their inversion as an attack against the monarchy; luckily, that action was never taken. The helmet was not a new element for Gaudí, as he had used it some years earlier to top the entrance gates to the Parc de la Ciutadella. He collaborated on that project as an assistant to Josep Fontserè, who was responsible for the design and execution of the gardens. Gaudí also designed elements of the waterfall and the stone balustrade around the monument to Aribau.

Between 1879 and 1881 he worked on what is today the Parish Church of Sant Pacià at no. 27, Carrer de les Monges, in the Sant Andreu de Palomar district, designing the flooring, altar, and tabernacle. The latter two were destroyed by fire during the Setmana Tràgica, or Tragic Week, riots of 1909. The design he made for the floor was based on the Roman mosaic technique.

Cast-iron and bronze lamppost, crowned by a helmet symbolising the god Mercury, in the Plaça Reial.

Inventory of No Longer Existing Works in Barcelona

Inventory of the Most Important Extant Projects Outside Barcelona

Fortunately, only lesser Barcelona works were destroyed. Here follows the list of the most interesting:

1879

Decoration of the Farmàcia Gibert, on the corner of Plaça de Catalunya and Fontanella

1883–1885

Comillas: El Capricho

1902

Part of the interior decor of Bar Torino, on Passeig de Gràcia/Gran Via

1887–1893

Astorga: The Episcopal Palace

1904

Doorway for the Chalet Graner, Carrer de la Immaculada, 44–46

1891–1892

León: La Casa de los Botines

1903–1914

Palma de Mallorca: restoration of the Cathedral

Tallers Badia, industrial nave, Carrer Nàpols, 278

Part of the interior decor of the Sala Mercè, La Rambla, 122

The standard for the Locksmiths Guild

1

2

3

4

1.
Comillas
El Capricho

2.
Astorga
The Episcopal Palace

3.
León
Casa de los Botines

4.
Palma de Mallorca
Restoration of the
Cathedral

PARC DEL
CASTELL DE
L'ORENETA
RONDA DE DALT
**Bellesguard,
la Casa Figueras**
RONDA DE DALT
RONDA DE DALT
c. DE DANTE ALIGHIERI
PG. DE LA REINA ELISENDA
PG. AV. DEL TIBIDABO
PG. DE SANT GERVASI
PARC DE
LA CREUETA
DEL COLL
c. DEL LLOBREGÓS
AV. DE PEDRALBES
VIA AUGUSTA
PG. DE LA BONANOVA
PL. DE LA
BONANOVA
c. DE BALMES
AV. DE LA REPÚBLICA ARGENTINA
AV. DE L'HOSPITAL MILITAR
RAMBLA DEL CARMEL
TURÓ DEL
PUTGET
PARC DEL
CARMEL
Park
Güell
PARC DEL
CASTELL DE
PAVELLONS
**Pavellons
Finca Güell**
Parc del
Palau Reial
de Pedralbes
**Col·legi de
les Teresianes**
RONDA DEL GENERAL MITRE
PARC DE
MONTEROLS
Parc Güell
VIA AUGUSTA
**Porta de la
finca Miralles**
c. DE GANDUXER
PL. DE
LESSEPS
PARC DEL
GUINARDÓ
GRAN VIA DE CARLES III
AV. DE SARRIÀ
AV. DIAGONAL
VIA AUGUSTA
Casa Vicens
TRAVESSERA DE DALT
c. DE L'ESCORIAL
PARC DE
LES AIGÜES
TURÓ
PARC
c. DE MUNTANER
c. DE BALMES
AV. DEL PRÍNCEP D'ASTÚRIES
c. DE GRÀCIA
c. DEL TORRENT DE L'OLLA
RONDA DEL GUINARDÓ
TRAV. DE LES CORTS
PL. DE
LES CORTS
PL. DE
FRANCESC
MACIÀ
c. D'ARIBAU
c. DE BALMES
TRAVESSERA DE GRÀCIA
c. DE PI I MARGALL
HOSPITAL DE
LA SANTA CREU
I SANT PAU
c. DE BRASIL
AV. DE MADRID
c. DE SANTS
c. DE NUMÀNCIA
c. DE LONDRES
c. DE JOSEP TARRADELLAS
c. DE PARÍS
AV. DIAGONAL
c. DE SANT ANTONI MARIA CLARET
c. DE CÒRSEGA
AV. DE GAUDÍ
c. DE CÒRSEGA
c. DE PROVENÇA
c. DEL ROSSELLÓ
PL. DELS
PAÏSOS
CATALANS
c. D'ENTENÇA
AV. DE ROMA
c. DEL COMTE D'URGELL
c. DE MALLORCA
c. DE BALMES
PG. DE GRÀCIA
**Casa Milà,
La Pedrera**
PL. MOSSÈN JACINT
VERDAGUER
c. DE SARDENYA
**Temple de la
Sagrada Família**
PARC DE
L'ESPANYA
INDUSTRIAL
c. DE TARRAGONA
c. D'ARAGÓ
c. DE VALÈNCIA
AV. DIAGONAL
c. DE CARTAGENA
Parc de
Joan Miró
(Escorxador)
c. DEL CONSELL DE CENT
Casa Batlló
PG. DE SANT JOAN
PG. DE ROGER DE FLOR
c. DE LA DIPUTACIÓ
PL. DE LES
GLÒRIES
CATALANES
PL.
D'ESPANYA
GRAN VIA DE LES CORTS CATALANES
PL. DE
TETUAN
c. DE CASP
c. DE SEPÚLVEDA
c. DE PELAI
Casa Calvet
c. D'AUSIÀS MARC
c. D'ÀLABA
AV. MISTRAL
c. DE SANT ANTONI
PL. DE
CATALUNYA
RONDA DE SANT PERE
RONDA DE SANT ANTONI
RONDA DE SANT PERE
PARC DE
L'ESTACIÓ
DEL NORD
AV. MERIDIANA
c. DE LLEIDA
RONDA DE SANT PAU
VIA LAIETANA
c. DELS ALMOGÀVERS
c. DE PERE IV
AV. DEL PARAL·LEL
LA RAMBLA
c. DE PUJADES
AV. DE L'ESTADI
c. DE SANT PAU
c. DE FERRAN
c. DE LA PRINCESA
PG. DE PICASSO
c. DE LA MARINA
c. DE LLULL
c. NOU DE LA RAMBLA
Palau Güell
**Fanals de la
Plaça Reial**
PARC
DE LA
CIUTADELLA
MONTJUÏC
**Fanals del
Govern Civil**
AV. D'ICÀRIA
PG. DE COLOM
RONDA DEL LITORAL
RONDA DEL LITORAL

MEDITERRANEAN SEA

The Works: Illustrations and Comentaries

Casa Vicens

1878–1888

Carrer de les Carolines, 18–24
Gràcia District

Detail of the palmetto-leaf fence
on the principal facade.

Light fixture and ceiling decoration of the gallery adjacent to the dining room.

Casa Vicens and its site as originally conceived; fortunately, none were too significant. Those undertaken by the architect Joan B. de Serra Martínez in 1925–26 were actually supervised by Gaudí. At that time the wall and railing that enclosed the property were removed. Fragments of the railing are preserved in the Park Güell, the Museu Güell, and the school of the same name. In 1946 part of the garden was sold for the development of a block of flats, and in 1962 a small temple on the grounds dedicated to Santa Rita was razed for the construction of additional flats. Casa Vicens was awarded the prestigious annual Barcelona City Hall Prize in 1927.

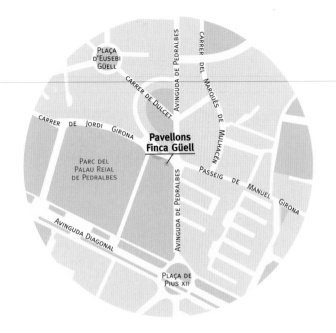

PLAÇA
D'EUSEBI
GÜELL

CARRER DE DULCET

CARRER DE JORDI GIRONA

AVINGUDA DE PEDRALBES

CARRER DEL MARQUÈS DE MULHACÉN

**Pavellons
Finca Güell**

PARC DEL
PALAU REIAL
DE PEDRALBES

PASSEIG DE MANUEL GIRONA

AVINGUDA DE PEDRALBES

AVINGUDA DIAGONAL

PLAÇA DE
PIUS XII

The Güell Estate Pavilions
1884–1887

Avinguda de Pedralbes, 7
Carrer de Manuel Girona
Sarrià / Sant Gervasi District

*Detail of the exterior wall
of the caretaker's lodge.*

*An ornamental detail
characterised by a
curiously naf accent.*

Viaducts, built of stone excavated on the site, enabled Gaudi to create a network of roadways that disrupted the landscape as little as possible.

national monument; and in 1984 it was included by UNESCO in the World Art Heritage list. The Amics de Gaudí association was able to acquire the architect's house in 1961. They established their headquarters there and in 1963 opened a museum. It primarily displays furniture, including pieces from Casa Calvet and Casa Batlló. The museum also possesses works by painter Aleix Clapés and sculptor Carles Mani, both of whom were among Gaudí's collaborators.

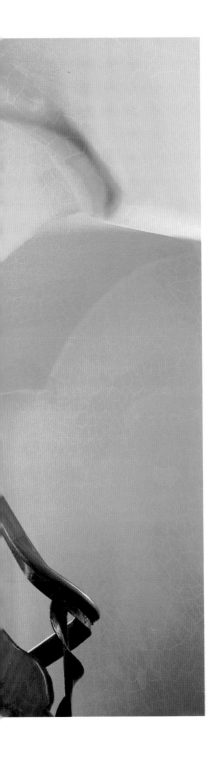

The undulations in this ceiling herald those of Casa Milà.

natural light. While the rear facade is not spectacular, it merits contemplation due to the effect Gaudí achieved in the pattern of solids and voids, and the multicoloured ornamentation. The recently restored attic is a spectacular space in which the potency of the exposed structure, the graceful parabolic arches, is revealed. Gaudí's sculptural treatment of chimney groups such as these has evolved from Palau Güell and culminates at Casa Milà. Here the chimneys are decorated with patterns of brightly coloured tiles.

The ground-floor level of Casa Batlló has recently been converted into a space which can be hired for meetings, conventions, and all manner of social functions. If we want certain old buildings to stay alive, we must refurbish and adapt them to new uses. In this case, the people of Barcelona and others who appreciate Gaudí's work now have the opportunity to visit a private property that had been closed to them.

While the cost of altering Casa Batlló was much higher than anticipated, due to Gaudí's penchant for designing while building, and while Batlló knew from personal experience that dealing with Gaudí required infinite patience, as he was strong-minded and often prickly, he still recommended the architect to his friend and business partner Milà, who had also decided to build a house on Passeig de Gràcia. And so it was that in 1906, as he finishing Casa Batlló, Gaudí began work on Casa Milà, which the people of Barcelona quickly christened La Pedrera, The Quarry.

Doors in Batllò apartment.

The hearth provides an unexpected private space.

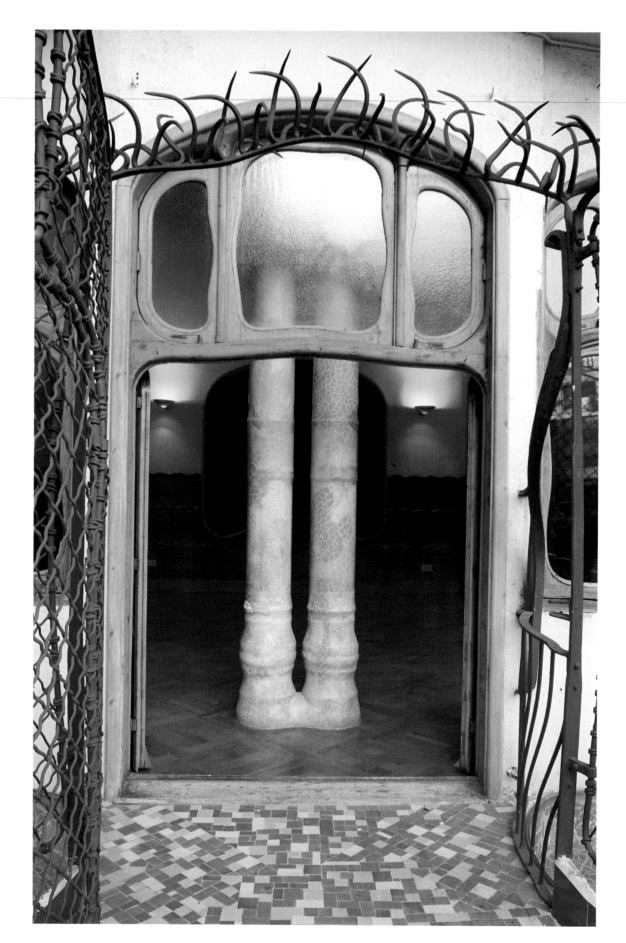